KILLER DINOSAURS
Theropods

Clare Hibbert

Enslow Publishing
101 W. 23rd Street
Suite 240
New York, NY 10011
USA
enslow.com

Published in 2019 by Enslow Publishing, LLC
101 W. 23rd Street, Suite 240, New York, NY 10011

Cataloging-in-Publication Data

Names: Hibbert, Clare.
Title: Killer Dinosaurs: Theropods / Clare Hibbert.
Description: New York : Enslow Publishing, 2019. | Series: Dino explorers | Includes glossary
and index.
Identifiers: ISBN 9781978500051 (pbk.) | ISBN 9781978500044 (library bound) | ISBN
9781978500068 (6 pack.) | ISBN 9781978500075 (ebook)
Subjects: LCSH: Saurischia--Juvenile literature. | Carnivorous animals, Fossil--Juvenile
literature. | Paleontology--Jurassic--Juvenile literature.
Classification: LCC QE862.S3 H53 2019 | DDC 567.912--dc23

Printed in the United States of America

To Our Readers: We have done our best to make sure all website addresses
in this book were active and appropriate when we went to press. However,
the author and the publisher have no control over and assume no
liability for the material available on those websites or on any websites
they may link to. Any comments or suggestions can be sent by email to
customerservice@enslow.com.

Excerpts and articles have been reproduced with the permission of the
copyright holders.

CONTENTS

The Dinosaur Age

Dinosaurs appeared around 225 million years ago (mya) and ruled the land for over 160 million years. At the same time (the Mesozoic Era), marine reptiles and pterosaurs ruled the oceans and skies.

Dinosaurs

This family tree shows when various dinosaurs appeared and how they were related. As new fossils are found, paleontologists often change their minds about the groupings.

Ornithischians

Dinosaurs suddenly died out 65 mya, along with marine reptiles, pterosaurs and many other animals. A huge meteorite probably hit Earth, throwing up dust that blocked out the Sun for months.

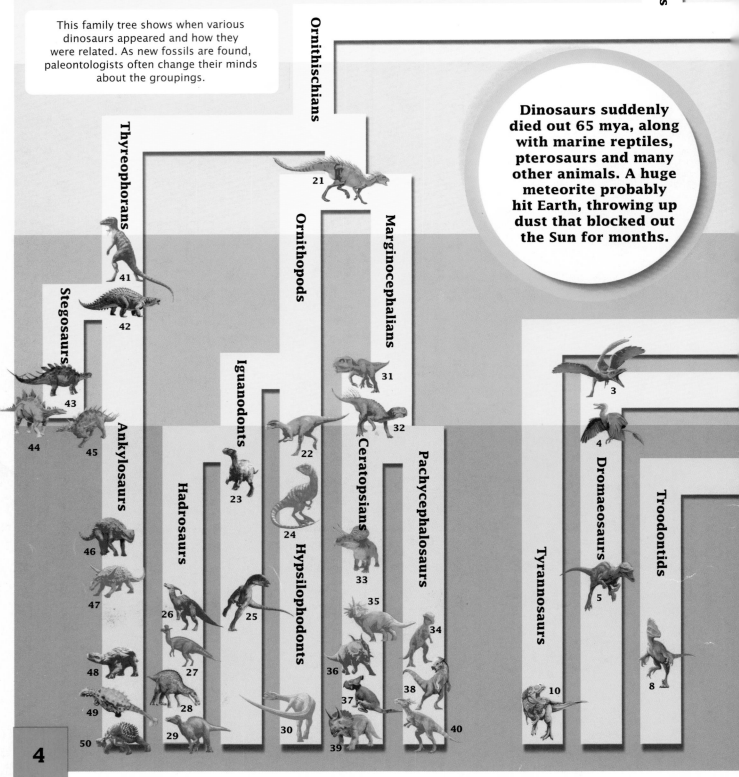

Thyreophorans

Stegosaurs

Ornithopods

Marginocephalians

Iguanodonts

Ankylosaurs

Hadrosaurs

Hypsilophodonts

Ceratopsians

Pachycephalosaurs

Dromaeosaurs

Troodontids

Tyrannosaurs

Saurischians

Theropods

Allosaurs

Sauropods

Prosauropods

Diplodocids

Spinosaurs

Titanosaurs

Therizinosaurs

Triassic
251–206 mya

Jurassic
206–145 mya

Cretaceous
145-65 mya

Herrerasaurus

One of the earliest carnivorous dinosaurs, *Herrerasaurus* lived in South America at the end of the Triassic period. There were many plant-eaters in its jungle habitat, but few dinosaurs. The main predators were archosaurs and early mammals called synapsids.

Close Relatives

Paleontologists have argued about *Herrerasaurus*'s place in the dinosaur family tree. Some count it as a primitive theropod (two-legged, carnivorous dinosaur). Others say it cannot be a theropod because it does not have opposable thumbs. They place *Herrerasaurus* in a group of its own.

Herrerasaurus was a speedy runner, thanks to its strong back legs.

From the Same Rocks

The first *Herrerasaurus* fossils were found in rocky mountains outside the city of San Juan in northwestern Argentina in 1959. The species is named after the farmer who discovered it, Victorino Herrera. The dinosaur *Eoraptor* was later found in the same rocks. Its name means "dawn lizard," and both these hunters were around at the very beginning of the dinosaur age.

*Eoraptor*s pause for a drink in their swampy forest home.

PERIOD	TRIASSIC	JURASSIC	CRETACEOUS	AGE OF MAMMALS	

231

MILLIONS OF YEARS AGO
251 206 145 65 present

Name: *Herrerasaurus*
(Her-RARE-uh-SAWR-us)
Family: Herrerasauridae
Height: 5 feet (1.5 m)
Length: 10 feet (3 m)
Weight: 460 pounds (210 kg)

DINOSAUR PROFILE

Herrerasaurus used sight and sound to find prey.

This small, stocky reptile is a rhynchosaur. Its beaky mouth clips off plant stems to eat.

Front legs had grasping, curved claws.

The first complete *Herrerasaurus* skull was discovered in 1988. Before then, paleontologists had to work from fragments.

Allosaurus

Late Jurassic North America was home to *Allosaurus*, one of the best-known carnivorous dinosaurs. Paleontologists have more fossils of *Allosaurus* to study than of any other dinosaur. The first were found in the late 19th century. The bones had honeycombed holes to make them lighter, just like birds' bones today. *Allosaurus* was given its name, which means "different lizard," because no other dinosaur fossils at that time had those holes.

Famous Fossils

Swiss fossil hunter Kirby Siber and his team of dinosaur experts were responsible for finding two of the most complete *Allosaurus* specimens. Discovered in Wyoming in 1991, the skeleton of "Big Al" is 95 percent complete. The specimen was not fully grown and probably died of a bone infection. Five years later the team found an even more complete *Allosaurus*, which they named "Big Al Two." Its skull showed signs of injuries that had healed.

On Location

There are five known species of *Allosaurus*. Four were discovered in the Morrison Formation, a band of Late Jurassic rock in the western United States. The other comes from western Portugal's Lourinhã Formation.

The long tail stuck out behind for balance.

PERIOD	TRIASSIC	JURASSIC	CRETACEOUS	AGE OF MAMMALS
		● 152		

MILLIONS OF YEARS AGO
251 — 206 — 145 — 65 — present

Name: *Allosaurus* (AL-uh-SAWR-us)
Family: Allosauridae
Height: 16.5 feet (5 m)
Length: 40 feet (12 m)
Weight: 3 tons (2.7 t)

DINOSAUR PROFILE

This *Allosaurus* skeleton is posed to take on *Stegosaurus*.

Thick, sturdy legs supported its heavy bulk.

Allosaurus had long claws for gripping flesh.

Allosaurus fed on carrion or its own kills.

Archaeopteryx

Birdlike *Archaeopteryx* lived in what is now southern Germany around 150 million years ago. For many years it was the oldest-known bird, but in recent decades earlier feathered dinosaurs have been discovered. *Archaeopteryx* had flight feathers for gliding.

Germany in the Late Jurassic

The landscape where *Archaeopteryx* lived was made up of low-lying islands among bodies of water, called lagoons. These lagoons had become separated from the nearby Tethys Ocean. When they dried up, the mud turned into limestone. Creatures that had sunk to the bottom were preserved as fossils.

Some experts think *Archaeopteryx*'s wrists were not flexible enough for powered flight.

Archaeopteryx was about the same size as a raven. It hunted frogs, lizards, dragonflies, and beetles.

Archaeopteryx's teeth were sharp and cone-shaped.

Flapping its wings while it was running helped *Archaeopteryx* to move faster.

Name: *Archaeopteryx*
(Ar-kee-OP-ter-ix)
Family: Archaeopterygidae
Length: 1 foot (0.3 m)
Wingspan: 1.7 feet (0.5 m)
Weight: 2.2 pounds (1 kg)

DINOSAUR PROFILE

Mesozoic dragonflies were huge, with wingspans of up to 2.5 feet (0.8 m).

Archaeopteryx means "ancient wing."

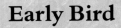

Early Bird

The first feathered dinosaur ever discovered, *Archaeopteryx* was nicknamed the "first bird." It was clearly an early ancestor of birds because of its wing and tail feathers. However, it also had reptilian features—a long, bony tail, large hand claws, and jaws lined with sharp teeth.

An *Archaeopteryx* skeleton preserved in limestone

11

Microraptor

The trees of Early Cretaceous China were home to *Microraptor*, a small, four-winged dromaeosaur. Like *Archaeopteryx*, it is one of the missing links between dinosaurs and birds. It probably used its wings to glide and parachute, rather than truly fly.

Microraptor stretched out its limbs and tail to be as aerodynamic as possible.

Speedy Killer

Microraptor was an opportunist—in other words, it ate whatever prey came its way. It must have been an agile, speedy hunter. *Microraptor* fossils show the remains of small mammals, birds, and even fish inside its gut. One bird meal had been swallowed whole.

Skeleton Specimens

Microraptor was discovered in 2000 in the Jiufotang Formation, a layer of rock in Liaoning, northeastern China. During the Early Cretaceous, Liaoning was warm and swampy. Rocks from that time contain the fossilized remains of many creatures, including other feathered dinosaurs. So far, hundreds of *Microraptor* specimens have been found.

Microraptor had fine, delicate bones.

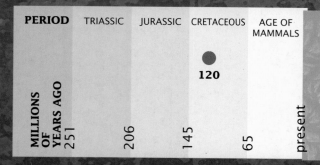

PERIOD	TRIASSIC	JURASSIC	CRETACEOUS	AGE OF MAMMALS
MILLIONS OF YEARS AGO	251	206	145 ● 120	65 present

Name: *Microraptor* (MY-kro-rap-tor)
Family: Dromaeosauridae
Length: 2.1 feet (0.6 m)
Wingspan: 3 feet (0.9 m)
Weight: 1.4 pounds (0.6 kg)

DINOSAUR PROFILE

Experts think *Microraptor* had gleaming, blackish feathers. Like starlings, it was iridescent, appearing different in different lights.

Microraptor hunted small, fast prey including birds.

Microraptor's teeth were serrated on only one side.

Microraptor means "small one who seizes." It used its hand-claws to grip meat or branches.

13

Deinonychus

The dromaeosaur *Deinonychus* lived in North America during the Early Cretaceous. It probably hunted in packs to bring down prey much larger than itself. Its name means "terrible claw" and its killer weapon was the sickle-shaped claw on its second toe.

Dangerous Family

Dromaeosaurs were formidable hunters. *Deinonychus* was medium-sized, about as large as a wolf. Its cousin *Utahraptor*, also from North America, was one of the largest species. It stood as tall as a person and was around 20 feet (6 m) long.

Working together, a team of *Deinonychus* could kill a juvenile *Tenontosaurus*. An adult was probably too large for them to attack.

In a Flap

Like all dromaeosaurs, *Deinonychus* had feathers. Experts believe that feathers evolved from reptilian scales that had frayed and grown fluffy. They helped dinosaurs to stay warm. In time, feathers were used for display, too. It is possible that *Deinonychus* juveniles could even fly from danger by flapping their arms.

PERIOD	TRIASSIC	JURASSIC	CRETACEOUS	AGE OF MAMMALS

MILLIONS OF YEARS AGO: 251   206   145   110   65   present

Name: *Deinonychus*
(Dye-NON-ik-us)
Family: Dromaeosauridae
Height: 4 feet (1.2 m)
Length: 11.2 feet (3.4 m)
Weight: 187 pounds (85 kg)

DINOSAUR PROFILE

Tenontosaurus, the most common plant-eater in its habitat, was often hunted by Deinonychus.

Deinonychus's hooked, second toe was about 5 inches (13 cm) long.

Deinonychus's killing method was to stab prey with its claws and then wait for it to bleed to death.

Deinonychus gripped its prey firmly with its claws. A kick could not shake it off.

Spinosaurus

The largest and longest carnivorous dinosaur, *Spinosaurus* lived in North Africa during the Cretaceous. Its pointed, crocodilian snout was perfectly shaped for snapping up fish, but this theropod also fed on dinosaurs and other land animals.

Species and Specimens

Only a handful of fairly complete *Spinosaurus* specimens have been found—and one of those was destroyed in bombing raids on Munich, Germany, during World War II. Most dinosaur experts recognize just one species, which they call *Spinosaurus aegyptiacus* ("Egyptian spine lizard").

Sail or Hump?

Most paleontologists believe that the spines along *Spinosaurus*'s back held up a large sail of skin. A few have another theory—that the spines supported a fatty hump, like a camel's. Either structure could have helped *Spinosaurus* to regulate its temperature, and either could have been used for display, to communicate with other dinosaurs.

Spinosaurus had a series of tall spines sticking out of its backbone. Most experts agree this supported a sail.

PERIOD	TRIASSIC	JURASSIC	CRETACEOUS	AGE OF MAMMALS
MILLIONS OF YEARS AGO	251	206	145	● 105	65	present

Name: *Spinosaurus* (SPY-nuh-SAWR-us)
Family: Spinosauridae
Height: 20 feet (6 m)
Length: 52.5 feet (16 m)
Weight: 9.9 tons (9 t)

DINOSAUR PROFILE

Giganotosaurus

When *Giganotosaurus* was discovered in Argentina in 1993, the 39-foot- (12-m-) long carnivore was thought to be the largest theropod in the southern hemisphere—and possibly even the world. Its name means "giant southern lizard."

On the Run

Giganotosaurus is known from preserved tracks and fossilized bones. Experts have been able to work out how fast it could run by considering its size and looking at the spacing between its footprints. Its top speed was probably around 31 miles (50 km) per hour. By comparison, *Tyrannosaurus rex* (pages 24–25) could reach only 25 miles (40 km) per hour.

Giganotosaurus

The Carcharodonts

Giganotosaurus was one of the carcharodonts, a group of dinosaurs named after the theropod *Carcharodontosaurus*, which lived in North Africa during the Late Cretaceous. Their sharp, serrated teeth resemble those of the great white shark, *Carcharodon*. Both *Giganotosaurus* and *Carcharodontosaurus* had a gigantic skull with bony ridges overhanging the eyes, massive jaws, and long teeth.

Carcharodontosaurus

PERIOD	TRIASSIC	JURASSIC	CRETACEOUS	AGE OF MAMMALS
MILLIONS OF YEARS AGO	251	206	145	65	present

98

Name: *Giganotosaurus* (JIG-an-oh-tuh-SAWR-us)
Family: Carcharodontosauridae
Height: 23 feet (7 m)
Length: 39 feet (12 m)
Weight: 8 tons (7.3 t)

DINOSAUR PROFILE

Giganotosaurus had low, horn-like projections on the bones above and in front of its eyes—just like *Carcharodontosaurus*.

Giganotosaurus had a weaker biting force than *T. rex*, but could snap its jaws shut more quickly.

Giganotosaurus was the apex (top) predator in its habitat.

Giganotosaurus's skull was about 6 feet (1.8 m) long.

Giganotosaurus had powerful, muscular back legs.

Troodon

Birdlike *Troodon* lived across North America in the Late Cretaceous. Its name means "wounding teeth." When it was first discovered in 1856 it was known from just one fossil, a small and extremely sharp tooth.

Clever Carnivore

Troodon is sometimes described as the most intelligent dinosaur. Compared to other dinosaurs its size, it probably was. Its brain was about six times heavier than others. However, it was only as large as an emu's brain today, so *Troodon* couldn't have been *that* smart.

Troodon preyed on other dinosaurs, such as young hadrosaurs. It also hunted small mammals and lizards.

Neat Nests

Troodon laid its eggs in bowl-shaped nests over a period of about a week. Just like ostriches today, it is likely that the males and females took turns sitting on the nest to keep the eggs warm. A typical nest contained between 16 and 24 eggs.

Part of a nest of *Troodon* eggs, preserved in rock.

Troodon had binocular vision—forward-pointing eyes that allowed it to judge distances.

Troodon's covering of feathers kept its body warm.

Troodon used its jaws, hands, or feet to grip prey.

PERIOD	TRIASSIC	JURASSIC	CRETACEOUS	AGE OF MAMMALS
			77	

MILLIONS OF YEARS AGO
251 · 206 · 145 · 65 · present

Name: *Troodon*
(TRO-uh-don)
Family: Troodontidae
Height: 3 feet (0.9 m)
Length: 7.9 feet (2.4 m)
Weight: 110 pounds (50 kg)

DINOSAUR PROFILE

Therizinosaurus

Unlike most other theropods, *Therizinosaurus* was not a meat-eater. Its diet was mostly made up of plants, although it may have also fed on insects and small animals. Its name, meaning "scythe lizard," comes from the three enormous, slashing claws on each hand.

Therizinosaurs

Therizinosaurus has given its name to a group of plant-eating theropods called the therizinosaurs. Others include *Beipiaosaurus*, *Alxasaurus*, and *Erlikosaurus*. As well as their long claws, they were distinguished by their long necks, broad, four-toed feet, and leaf-shaped teeth.

Therizinosaurus was covered in light feathers.

Fossilized teeth belonging to *Erlikosaurus*.

Unlike most theropods, therizinosaurs had four toes, not three.

70

Name: *Therizinosaurus*
(THAIR-uh-zeen-uh-SAWR-us)
Family: Therizinosauridae
Height: 12 feet (3.7 m)
Length: 33 feet (10 m)
Weight: 5.5 tons (5 t)

DINOSAUR PROFILE

Therizinosaurus's 3.3-foot- (1-m-) long claws could defend against predators.

Therizinosaurus had a bulky body. It needed a large stomach for digesting plant matter.

Clever Claws

Therizinosaurus lived in what is now Mongolia at the end of the Cretaceous. Its claws helped it to fend off predators such as *Tarbosaurus*, sometimes known as the Asian *T. rex*. The claws had other uses, too. Perhaps they cut down vegetation or allowed the dinosaur to "fish" for termites in termite mounds.

Being tall enabled *Therizinosaurus* to reach to the highest branches.

Tyrannosaurus

One species of *Tyrannosaurus* is more famous than any other dinosaur: *Tyrannosaurus rex*, or "king of the tyrant lizards." It inhabited North America at the end of the Cretaceous. For a long time, it was the largest known land carnivore. Today, that title goes to *Spinosaurus* (pages 16–17).

Search for Meat

Tyrannosaurus had binocular vision, which meant that it could locate prey with great accuracy. It could also move fairly quickly, thanks to its muscular back legs. Once it reached its prey, it tore into its flesh with powerful jaws. *Tyrannosaurus*'s teeth could easily crush through bone. Teeth were different sizes, but the longest were about 6 inches (15 cm).

One *Tyrannosaurus* sinks its teeth into another's neck.

Life in a Pack

Trackways in Canada show that—at least some of the time—*Tyrannosaurus* hunted in packs. As in wolf packs today, rival males probably fought each other to be pack leader. *Tyrannosaurus* would have used its fearsome jaws not only to kill prey, but to attack rivals.

PERIOD	TRIASSIC	JURASSIC	CRETACEOUS	AGE OF MAMMALS
MILLIONS OF YEARS AGO	251	206	145	67 65 present

Name: *Tyrannosaurus* (Tye-RAN-uh-SAWR-us)
Family: Tyrannosauridae
Height: 18 feet (5.5 m)
Length: 39 feet (12 m)
Weight: 6.7 tons (6.1 t)

DINOSAUR PROFILE

Tyrannosaurus is estimated to have been able to deliver a stronger bite than any other land animal.

Tyrannosaurus probably had feathers for warmth.

Tail held out behind for balance.

Tyrannosaurus walked on slim, birdlike feet. Each foot had three 7-inch- (18-cm-) long claws.

Tyrannosaurus's arms were short but powerful. The dinosaur scavenged and hunted.

Fun Facts

Now that you have discovered some amazing killer dinosaurs, boost your knowledge with these 10 quick facts about them!

By studying *Herrerasaurus* coprolites (fossils of dung!), scientists know that this carnivore crunched up and digested bone.

Allosaurus was very common. Up to three-quarters of the theropod fossils from the Morrison Formation in the United States belong to *Allosaurus*.

The first *Archaeopteryx* fossil was found in 1859—the same year that Charles Darwin published his theory of evolution by natural selection.

Microraptor was not the only four-winged dinosaur. *Changyuraptor*, also from Cretaceous China, was the largest, measuring 4.3 feet (1.3 m) from nose to tail.

Deinonychus was first discovered in 1931—but it was not actually given a name until 1969.

The tallest of the neural spines along *Spinosaurus*'s back were at least 5.4 feet (1.6 m) long.

Giganotosaurus had a close cousin, *Mapusaurus*, which lived in Argentina at the same time and was just as large.

Troodon's relatively large eyes let in plenty of light. It could hunt at dawn, at dusk, or even in the middle of the night.

Therizinosaurs probably nested in groups. Seventeen clutches of eggs were found close to each other in the Gobi Desert, China, in 2013.

Tyrannosaurus's 4-foot- (1.2-m-) long jaw contained up to 58 serrated teeth.

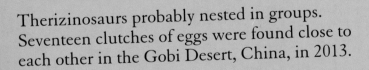

Your Questions Answered

Our scientific knowledge and technologies are constantly improving, which helps paleontologists uncover more and more information about dinosaurs. Each question answered leads to many new ones being asked, and it is the quest of scientists to keep searching for answers to give us the fullest possible picture of prehistoric life. Here are some fascinating questions we can now answer.

Which was the fastest dinosaur?

By studying the skeletons and working out the muscle structure of dinosaurs, scientists are able to calculate the speed at which each creature could run. They believe that one kind of theropod was the fastest: ornithomimids. Their name comes from the Greek for "bird mimics" (or "bird copiers"), because they look similar to today's large, flightless birds, such as ostriches. And similar to ostriches, the fastest ornithomimid, *Dromiceiomimus*, could probably reach speeds of up to 37 miles (60 km) per hour!

*The name **Dromiceiomimus** means "Emu mimic," because it looks similar to Australia's Emu—a relative of the ostrich.*

Do we know anything about dinosaurs' internal organs?

Because internal organs are formed from soft tissue, they usually decompose before the fossilization process has set in. As such, there is hardly any evidence of dinosaurs' internal organs. The most detailed find was a juvenile *Scipionyx*, whose fossil included traces of its windpipe, guts, and possibly liver.

Where did most theropods live?

Theropod fossils have been found on all continents, so we know they were widely distributed. However, while we know enough about them to be able to group and identify them, theropod fossils are rare. Not many have been found intact, and especially small theropods did not fossilize well due to their dainty, fragile bones. So finding multiple fossils in one location probably means that fossilizing conditions were ideal, rather than that theropods predominantly lived there.

Troodon *was light, quick, and agile, thanks to its hollow bones and feather coat.*

Which diseases did dinosaurs suffer from?

Judging by the fossils that have been studied so far, scientists believe that dinosaurs were healthier than humans are today! There may have been some diseases that only affected the soft tissue, and therefore can't be detected in fossils, but beyond that, dinosaurs had very little complaints. Most injuries have been found in large carnivores, such as *Tyrannosaurus rex*, as these animals would have been in combat a lot when hunting their prey. Dinosaurs rarely suffered from broken bones, and there is also little evidence of tumors and infections.

Tyrannosaurus rex *often suffered head and rib injuries when hunting prey.*

Glossary

allosaur A large theropod with a long, narrow skull, usually with ornamental horns or crests.

archosaur An animal whose skull has one hole between the eye socket and nostril and another at the back of the lower jaw. Dinosaurs, pterosaurs, crocodiles, and birds are all archosaurs.

carnivore A meat-eater.

carrion Rotting flesh from a dead animal.

Cretaceous period The time from 145 to 65 mya, and the third of the periods that make up the Mesozoic Era.

dromaeosaur A small theropod with an outsize claw on each back foot.

evolution The process by which one species changes into another over millions of years, by passing on particular characteristics from one generation to the next.

fossil The remains of an animal or plant that died long ago, preserved in rock.

hadrosaur Also known as a duck-billed dinosaur, an ornithopod with an especially beak-like mouth.

Jurassic period The time from 206 to 145 mya, and the second of the periods that make up the Mesozoic Era.

Mesozoic Era The period of geological time from 251 to 65 million years ago.

mya Short for "millions of years ago."

paleontologist A scientist who studies fossils.

predator An animal that hunts and eats other animals for food.

prey An animal that is hunted and eaten by other animals for food.

rhynchosaur A small, primitive reptile.

scavenge To eat carrion or leftover kills from other hunters.

serrated Having a notched, knife-like edge.

species One particular type of living thing. Members of the same species look similar and can produce offspring together.

spinosaur A specialist theropod with a long, narrow snout for eating fish.

synapsid A primitive mammal.

therizinosaur A large (probably plant-eating) theropod with huge hand claws.

theropod A bipedal saurischian dinosaur with sharp teeth and claws.

Triassic period The time from 251 to 206 mya, and the first of the periods that make up the Mesozoic Era.

troodontid A birdlike theropod with long legs and good senses.

tyrannosaur A large theropod with a huge head and relatively small arms.

wingspan The width of a flying animal's outstretched wings, from wing tip to wing tip.

Further Information

BOOKS

Holtz, Thomas R. Jr. *Digging for Tyrannosaurus rex.* North Mankato, MN: Capstone Press, 2015.

Miles, Liz. *Killer Dinosaurs.* New York, NY: Gareth Stevens Publishing, 2016.

Parker, Steve. *The Science of Killer Dinosaurs: The Bloodcurdling Truth About T. Rex and Other Theropods.* New York, NY: Franklin Watts, 2018.

Peterson, Megan Cooley. *Allosaurus and Its Relatives: The Need-to-Know Facts.* North Mankato, MN: Capstone Press, 2017.

Woodward, John. *Everything You Need to Know about Dinosaurs: and Other Prehistoric Creatures.* New York, NY: DK Publishing, 2014.

WEBSITES

discoverykids.com/category/dinosaurs/
This Discovery Kids site has tons of awesome information about dinosaurs, plus lots of fun games and exciting videos!

kids.nationalgeographic.com/explore/nature/dinosaurs/
Check out this National Geographic Kids site to learn more about dinosaurs.

www.amnh.org/explore/ology/paleontology
This website by the American Museum of Natural History is filled with dinosaur quizzes, information, and activities!

Index

A

Allosaurus 5, 8–9, 26
Alxasaurus 22
Archaeopteryx 5, 10–11, 12, 26
archosaur 6

B

Beipiaosaurus 22
bird 8, 10, 11, 12, 13, 20, 25, 28

C

Carcharodon 18
carcharodont 18
Carcharodontosaurus 18, 19
carnivore 6, 8, 16, 18, 20, 24, 26, 29
carrion 9
Changyuraptor 26
claw 7, 9, 11, 13, 14, 15, 22, 23, 25
coelacanth 17
Cretaceous period 4–5, 12, 14, 16, 18, 23, 24, 26

D

Deinonychus 5, 14–15, 26
dromaeosaur 4, 12–13, 14–15
Dromiceiomimus 28

E

egg 20, 27
Eoraptor 6
Erlikosaurus 22

F

feathers 10, 11, 12, 13, 14, 21, 22, 25, 29
fossil 4, 6, 8, 10, 12, 18, 20, 22, 26, 29

G

Giganotosaurus 5, 18–19, 27

H

hadrosaur 4, 20
Herrera, Victorino 6
Herrerasaurus 5, 6–7, 26
hunt 10, 13, 14, 15, 20, 24, 25, 27, 29

J

Jurassic period 4–5, 8, 10

L

lizard 6, 8, 10, 16, 18, 20, 22, 24

M

mammal 6, 12, 20
Mapusaurus 27
Microraptor 5, 12–13, 26

O

ornithomimids 28

P

predator 6, 19, 23, 29
prey 7, 12, 13, 14, 15, 20, 21, 24, 29

R

rhynchosaur 7

S

scavenge 25
Scipionyx 28
Siber, Kirby 8
Spinosaurus 5, 16–17, 24, 27
Stegosaurus 5, 9
synapsid 6

T

Tarbosaurus 23
teeth 10, 11, 13, 18, 20, 22, 24, 27
Tenontosaurus 14, 15
termite 23
Therizinosaurus 5, 22–23
Triassic period 4–5, 6
Troodon 5, 20–21, 27, 29
Tyrannosaurus 5, 24–25, 27
Tyrannosaurus rex 18, 19, 23, 24, 29

U

Utahraptor 14

W

wing 10, 11, 12, 26